A Beastly Tale

Written by Sharon Wohl
Illustrated by Adam Byrne

A Better Way of Learning
Creator of The Phonics Game™

Copyright© 1998 by A Better Way of Learning, Inc. All rights reserved. This publication, or any part thereof, may not be reproduced in any form or by any means, including electronic, photographic, or mechanical, or by any sound recording system, or by any device for storage and retrieval of information, without the written permission of the publisher.

Printed in the U.S.A.

A Better Way of Learning • www.phonicsgame.com

Out of a cave
In the dark and the fog,
Stamps a huge, brown beast
Midst the mire in the bog.

With his feet in the moss
And the muck and the mud,
He drags up the path
With a thump and a thud.

He stomps up the road
And soon reaches the town.
He slides on the stones
With a groan and a frown.

The boy by the cow
Sees the beast in the gloom.
He yells to the town
With a voice that shouts doom.

The men leave the tents.
A mob forms in the square.
Must they kill this big brute?
Will they try? Will they dare?

7.

The gypsy camp peers
At the beast that they see.
A loud voice shouts out,
"Lash the beast to a tree!"

9.

The beast, he cries out
With a loud and shrill scream.
He blows out his nose
With fire, smoke and hot steam.

Men ride up the hill
With news for the king.
He must tell them now
How to deal with this thing.

Gentle maid hears the tale,
And she seeks out the beast.
She consoles him and learns
Not to fear him the least.

"Please free him," she cries.
"He can help us with chores.
Let me train him and teach him
Down by the moors."

Eight weeks go by,
And the beast has a trade

He helps out a lot,
And the town's not afraid.

15.

So if you go down
To the road by the moor,
Greet the beast that helps out
At the king's huge front door.